AF270585

FRENCH BULLDOGS

by Elizabeth Andrews

Cody Koala

An Imprint of Pop!
popbooksonline.com

This book is filled with videos, puzzles, games, and more! Scan the QR codes* while you read, or visit the website below to make this book pop.

popbooksonline.com/frenchies

*Scanning QR codes requires a web-enabled smart device with a QR code reader app and a camera.

abdobooks.com

Published by Pop!, a division of ABDO, PO Box 398166, Minneapolis, Minnesota 55439. Copyright ©2023 by Abdo Consulting Group, Inc. International copyrights reserved in all countries. No part of this book may be reproduced in any form without written permission from the publisher. Cody Koala™ is a trademark and logo of Pop!.

Printed in the United States of America, North Mankato, Minnesota.

102022
012023

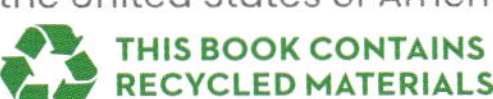 **THIS BOOK CONTAINS RECYCLED MATERIALS**

Cover Photo: Shutterstock Images
Interior Photos: Shutterstock Images
Editor: Grace Hansen
Series Designer: Colleen McLaren

Library of Congress Control Number: 2022941108

Publisher's Cataloging-in-Publication Data
Names: Andrews, Elizabeth, author.
Title: French bulldogs / by Elizabeth Andrews
Description: Minneapolis, Minnesota : Pop!, 2023 | Series: Dogs | Includes online resources and index.
Identifiers: ISBN 9781098243197 (lib. bdg.) | ISBN 9781098243890 (ebook)
Subjects: LCSH: French bulldogs--Juvenile literature. | Bulldog--Juvenile literature. | Toy dog breeds--Juvenile literature. | Domestic Dog--Juvenile literature.
Classification: DDC 636.72--dc23

Table of Contents

Chapter 1

Fancy Frenchies

The French bulldog's round muscular body, smooshed nose, and square head gives it the classic bulldog look. French bulldogs were **bred** to be lapdog-sized versions of the English bulldog.

Watch a video here!

English bulldog

French bulldog

French bulldogs have a smooth coat. They can be black, **brindle**, cream, or white in color. They can also have markings. Their black nose sits on the tip of their short, wrinkly **muzzle**.

A French bulldog's tail is naturally short. It can be straight or shaped like a corkscrew.

Along with their famous snout, Frenchies are known for their big bat-like ears. The ears sit wide on the

top of a big square head.
Short, sturdy legs hold up
these 16 to 28 pound (7.25–
12.7kg) dogs.

Chapter 2

Personality

French bulldogs are sweet, and easygoing. Because of these traits, Frenchies **adapt** well to new places and people. They also make good watchdogs. Frenchies mostly just want attention and love.

Learn more here!

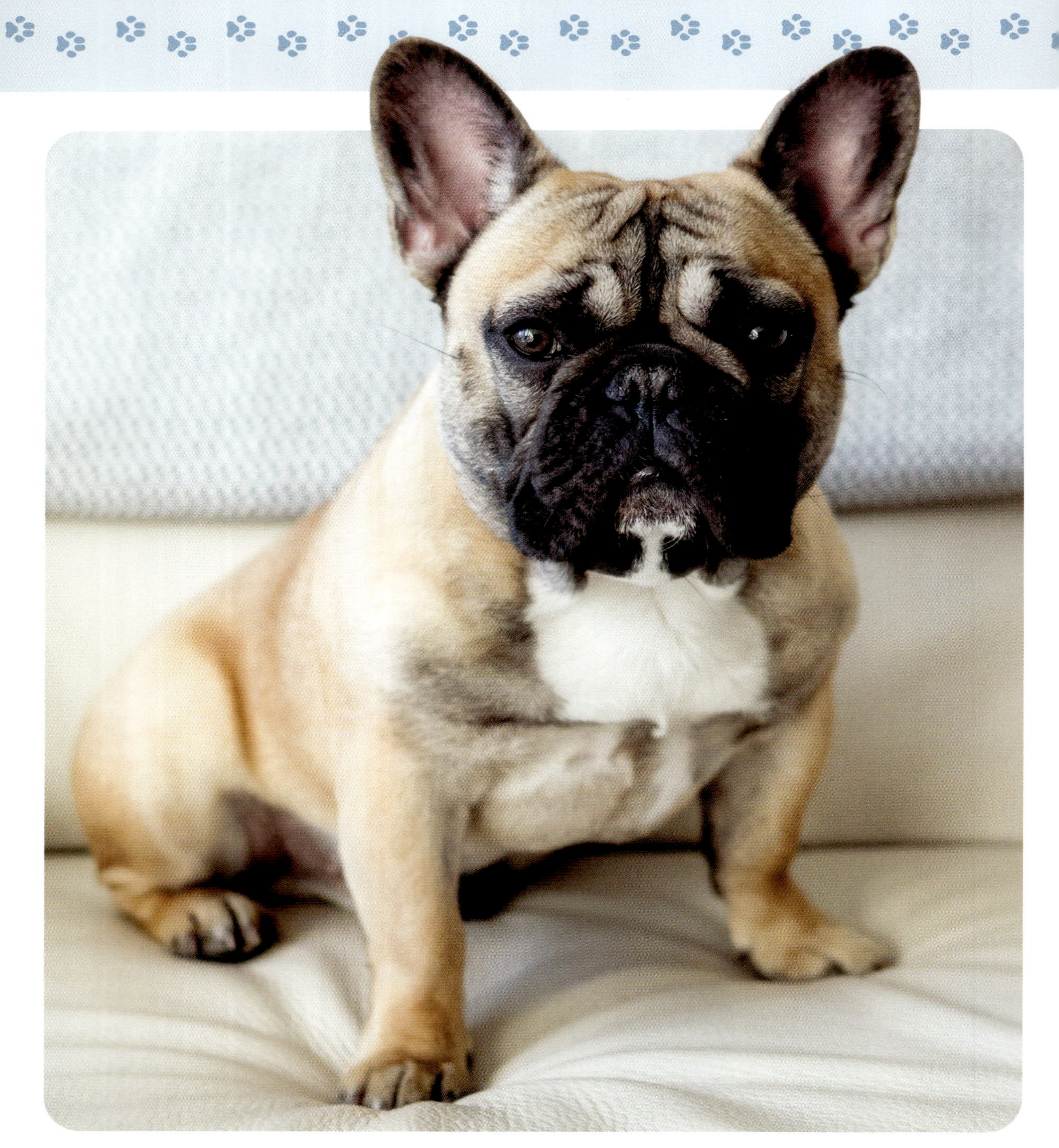

Frenchies can live in both big and small homes. They are good with children. They are very playful and easy to train.

Chapter 3

Pet Care

French bulldogs are easy to care for. They only need brushing once a week. Owners should keep their dog's face wrinkles clean and dry to avoid **infections**.

Explore links here!

French bulldog's short

muzzle makes breathing

in heat hard. Their activity

should be **monitored** during

hot weather. Frenchies can
handle short, slow walks.
They need a cool place
to rest.

Like all dogs, Frenchies should have fresh, clean water and healthy food. They need a leash and collar with identification tags. They should be taken to the vet at least once a year for checkups.

Chapter 4

Puppies

French bulldog puppies are born deaf and blind. They can hear and see at ten to 14 days old. Puppies begin walking at around three weeks old. At 12 weeks, they are ready for **adoption**!

Complete an
activity here!

Making Connections

Text-to-Self

French bulldogs were bred to be smaller versions of the English bulldog. Which bulldog would you want? Explain your answer.

Text-to-Text

Have you read any other books about a certain type of dog? What did that dog have in common with the French bulldog?

Text-to-World

French bulldogs were first bred in France. Can you think of different breeds that come from other countries?

Glossary

adapt – to change behavior so that it is easier to live in a particular place or situation

adoption – the act of accepting an animal as a pet and taking on the responsibility of it.

bred – developed to act and look a specific way, or serve a certain purpose.

brindle – a color pattern with streaks of red, brown, or black

infection – an illness caused by germs.

monitor – to watch closely and check on.

muzzle – the jaws and nose of an animal.

Index

Online Resources

popbooksonline.com

Thanks for reading this Cody Koala book!

This book is filled with videos, puzzles, games, and more! Scan the QR codes* while you read, or visit the website below to make this book pop.

popbooksonline.com/frenchies

*Scanning QR codes requires a web-enabled smart device with a QR code reader app and a camera.